MIXED BLESSINGS
The Special Child in Your School

by Erica Brown

The National Society (Church of England)
for Promoting Religious Education

Preface

Children with special educational needs of any kind are now educated in mainstream schools wherever possible. This integrated approach is a blessing, but a mixed one: it challenges the school in terms of its organisation, its teaching and the expertise of all who work there. In this practical guide, written for governors and staff in all types of maintained school – county, voluntary and grant-maintained – the author shows how schools can make the most of this duty and opportunity to provide the best possible education for all their children. There is guidance on legislation, technical terms, the responsibilities of governors, the rôle of parents, staffing and the curriculum, as well as useful sections on the kinds of learning difficulty and physical disability that cause children to have special educational needs. A chapter on the distinctive rôle of the Church school is included.

Erica Brown trained as a primary school teacher and taught for twenty years, fifteen of them in special schools. She is a national authority on special education, well known for her writings and training courses. Her publications include, in the National Society booklet series, ***Opening Their Eyes: Worship and RE with Children with Special Needs*** (1991) and, as co-author with Alan Brown, ***Primary School Worship*** (1992). She is co-editor of the journal ***Respect***.

Copyright © The National Society (Church of England) for Promoting Religious Education 1993

Printed by The Good News Press Limited, Ongar (0277) 362106

Contents

		Page
	Introduction	4
1.	Defining Special Educational Needs	6
2.	Understanding the Language of Special Education	9
3.	The Distinctive Rôle of the Church School	14
4.	Responsibilities of Governors	17
5.	Parents as Partners in their Child's Education	21
6.	The School Curriculum and Assessment of Children's Progress	24
7.	School Staffing	29
8.	Pupils with Specific Learning Difficulties: Types of Disability; Organising the Classroom; Glossary of Terms	33
9.	Questions for Governors	44
10.	Recent Government Policy	48
11.	Guide to Documents Concerning Special Educational Needs	50

Introduction

For pupils with special educational needs the last two decades have contained mixed blessings. At a time when the content and stance of education have been under critical review, and it is estimated that one in five of all pupils in mainstream education will experience some kind of learning difficulty, Church schools and others are faced with a challenge: to nurture, rather than to neglect, the education and spiritual development of persons who have greater difficulty in learning than normal.

In 1987 a House of Commons Select Committee reviewed the implementation of the 1981 Education Act and reported a wide variety of practice and provision across the country concerning the schooling of children with special educational needs. Since then the Education (No. 2) Act 1986 and the Education Reform Act 1988 have significantly altered the management of schools. At the time of writing the 1993 Education Bill proposes several changes which would affect pupils with special educational needs.

Few parents and educationalists would argue against the principles, especially that of integration rather than segregation, which have shaped recent recommendations, but there is a danger that the new legal framework could seriously marginalise children with special educational needs and lead to more segregation, not less, as schools face the reality that a child with learning difficulties is a more costly commodity than most and is less likely to boost published performance results. Certainly, as schools struggle to cope with the National Curriculum targets of attainment and assessment while simultaneously attempting to balance the budget, whole school policies to meet special needs could prove to be early casualties. Fortunately this scenario is not inevitable if people can maintain a sense of goodwill, trust, commitment and partnership within the education system.

Governors may at any time be called upon to give support to their school (including children, staff and parents) concerning the education of pupils with special educational needs. To be effective they will need to have some knowledge of the terminology and implications of special educational needs and a commitment to ensuring that, wherever possible, a child's needs can be met within an ordinary school. The teaching of pupils with special educational needs is not a totally different enterprise from that of teaching in general.

The aim of this booklet is to support teachers and governors as they respond to the challenge they face in meeting the needs of *all* the children in their school. The reader will find throughout an expressed commitment towards a 'collective responsibility' for children, regardless of their ability, background or circumstances. It is a booklet about attitude and action which has at its heart the belief that Church schools, and others, can be not only models of excellence in their teaching but also places where the *mixed blessings* of educating children are celebrated.

1 Defining Special Educational Needs

The concept of special educational needs is a changing one. People are coming to recognise that there is no clear-cut category of children who need special help or special education; many individuals will have some kind of learning difficulty during their lives.

During the last decade there has been frequent discussion and some significant legislation concerning those pupils who will at some time in their school life have greater difficulty in learning than others. Early attempts by educationalists to classify the characteristics of pupils with learning difficulties were strongly influenced by concepts about the genetic basis of intelligence and the result of intelligence testing. In recent years the incidence and understanding of special educational needs has altered. As a result of medical, economic and social changes certain disabilities now occur less frequently whereas others, like emotional and behavioural difficulties, are more common. The change in the pattern has sometimes been gradual and subtle, sometimes dramatic.

Linked with these changes has been a growing understanding of the complexity of learning difficulties. ***Special Educational Needs***, the report of the Committee of Enquiry into the Education of Handicapped Children and Young People, known as the Warnock Report (1978), suggested that learning difficulties might be divided into three categories: mild, moderate and severe. These categories referred to degrees of difficulty in learning and not to clearly defined groups of children.

The 1981 Education Act recognised a wide range of special educational needs, stressing that their definition was not linked to specific causes and is therefore relative to the needs of *all* children. The Act outlined three principles of special educational needs:

- all children have the right to education and common needs are pre-eminent. Disabilities and significant difficulties are variations in need, not categories of different 'types' of children.
- each child should be individually assessed so that where special educational provision is necessary this can be planned to meet identified needs.
- the ordinary school should be the setting for special education wherever possible.

During the decade since the 1981 Education Act and its implementation there has been a general recognition of the following:

- the needs of children with learning difficulties are not different in nature from those of other children. There are not two sorts of pupil: those with special educational needs and those without. Indeed children who may require special education often have more needs in common with other children than they have different ones.
- disabilities and difficulties vary widely in nature and degree, and special educational needs may be short- or long-term.
- the effects of disabilities are individual, and although they may be categorised in medical or psychological terms, the same categories are not necessarily helpful in describing special educational needs. Children will need individual assessment and individual statements of their specific needs and how these might be met within the education service.

Educationalists have had to categorise *the degrees of learning difficulty* experienced by children, for the purpose of providing an appropriate education. These may be summarised as:

Severe, profound or multiple learning difficulties
Children with these have poor intellectual ability as well as additional problems such as physical disability, poor health,

limited language, emotional disturbance. These children will require education in special schools or special classes in ordinary schools. Most pupils in this category display a limited capacity for academic work and they require a special curriculum to promote their personal and social development.

Moderate learning difficulties
This term applies to children whose ability is less limited but who have more difficulty in learning than most pupils due to factors such as school absence, unfortunate personal circumstances or inadequate environmental conditions. Most of these children can be educated in ordinary schools but they may require a modified curriculum.

Mild learning difficulties
Children with these do not have limited intellectual ability but are still at the beginning stages of reading and writing skills. Most of these pupils will achieve average attainment in practical subjects, although a large proportion may experience perceptual or emotional difficulties. They are generally educated within mainstream schools.

Physical or sensory disabilities
Many pupils with these will require education in a special school although some are very successfully integrated into mainstream schools where there are additional resources, especially if they are of average intellectual ability.

2 Understanding the Language of Special Education

The terminology of special education can form an artificial barrier between it and mainstream schooling. For this reason it is important that all who are involved in education should be aware of the definitions which are used. Some of those listed refer to specific types of special educational need, some to teaching methods and the school curriculum, others to organisations. The list is not definitive but it includes those terms most commonly used in policy documents and by the teaching profession.

Ability
The general intelligence of a child or competence in a specific subject or activity.

Ancillary Staff
See below, under Support Staff.

Assessment
The process of evaluating and measuring capabilities, skills and limitations through tests which may be medical, social and/or psychological. The term is also used to describe the procedures for formal examination of pupils who may need a statement of special educational needs (see also Statement of Special Educational Needs).

Basic Skills
Traditionally this term referred to the Three Rs – reading, writing and arithmetic. Less widely used since the implementation of the National Curriculum in 1988.

Circular
Policy statement issued by the DFE (Department for Education) to LEAs (Local Education Authorities). These documents do not themselves have the force of the law, but offer guidance on interpretation of the law.

Continuous Assessment
Regular and on-going evaluation of a child's progress. The results achieved may be used in examination results.

DES
See below, under DFE.

DFE
The Department for Education (DFE) came into being on 7 July 1992, replacing the Department of Education and Science (DES). It is responsible for all education, including special education, in England (the Welsh Office has this responsibility for Wales).

Dyslexia
The learning difficulty which some pupils encounter in the acquisition of reading and writing skills. Dyslexia is independent of intelligence and and may therefore occur over a wide range of measured intelligence. Dyslexia is sometimes called 'word blindness'.

Educational Psychologist
A professionally qualified teacher, usually with a degree in psychology and post-graduate qualifications in educational psychology. Educational Psychologists assess and advise on the intellectual, emotional, social and physical development of children. A child with a Statement of Special Educational Needs will have been assessed by an Educational Psychologist.

Emotional and Behavioural Disorders (EBD)
Behavioural difficulties which may hamper a child's learning. Formerly described as 'maladjustment.'

Exclusion
The temporary or permanent exclusion of a pupil from school on disciplinary or medical grounds.

Home-School Liaison Teacher
Teacher with responsibility for working with parents/carers of pupils who have special educational needs and for maintaining the links with other support services.

Home Tuition
Teaching at home for medical or other reasons where a child is unable to attend school. The service is at present provided by the LEA and 10 hours a week is the recommended minimum.

In-service Training (INSET)
Courses for employed teachers which aim to update professional expertise and skills. Since the School Teachers' Pay and Conditions Act 1987, five days per year of in-service training are compulsory for full-time teachers in schools. Sometimes also called staff training days.

Integration
The education of children with statements of special educational needs (for whatever reason) together with other children without statements of special educational needs in mainstream education.

Key Stages 1, 2, 3 and 4
The ages of 7, 11, 14, 16 when pupils are tested to ascertain what they have achieved in relation to the attainment targets set for those stages in the National Curriculum. Introduced by the Education Reform Act 1988.

LEAs
Local education authorities in England and Wales.

Learning Difficulty
Occurs when a child has significantly greater difficulty in learning than the majority of his or her peers. (see also Special Educational Needs)

National Curriculum
Curriculum prescribed by the Secretary of State for Education for teaching to all pupils in maintained mainstream and special schools under the Education Reform Act 1988.

National Curriculum Council (NCC)
A body established by the Education Reform Act 1988 to advise the Secretary of State for Education and to keep under review all aspects of the National Curriculum. NCC will be

incorporated with SEAC into SCAA (School Curriculum and Assessment Authority) in 1993.

Non-maintained Special Schools
Schools which are non profit-making and which operate under the Handicapped Pupils and Special Schools Regulations 1979. Some non-maintained special schools receive government grants and financial support from charities and trusts. Most pupils are referred to these schools by LEAs which are responsible for paying their fees.

Outreach
The provision of expert help in another setting e.g. special school teachers offering to support pupils in mainstream schools.

Remedial Class/Department
Remedial teaching strives to help pupils who have learning difficulties in mainstream schools. Such classes are often taught by a suitably qualified teacher. Pupils may be withdrawn from some lessons to attend remedial education or kept in a group apart from other children of the same age-group for full-time remedial teaching.

Residential School
A school at which children with special educational needs live and are taught.

School Curriculum and Assessment Authority (SCAA)
Replaces both the NCC and SEAC on 1 October 1993.

Schools Examinations and Assessment Council (SEAC)
A body set up by the Education Reform Act 1988 to advise the Secretary of State for Education and keep under review all aspects of assessment and examinations. Replaced the former Secondary Examinations Council, and will be incorporated into SCAA in 1993.

Special Educational Needs (SEN)
The term given to the needs of any child who has a learning difficulty which calls for special educational provision to be made. A pupil is considered to have a learning difficulty if

he/she has significantly greater difficulty in learning than the majority of children of the same age, or has a disability which either prevents or hinders him/her from making use of educational facilities of a kind generally provided in schools within the area of the local authority concerned for children of his/her age.

Special School
A school which specialises in providing education for the needs of pupils with specific learning difficulties or a combination of disabilities.

Special Unit
A unit attached to a mainstream school or special school to cater for pupils with specific educational needs.

Specific Learning Difficulty
The term usually describes the learning difficulty experienced by a child in one area of the curriculum e.g. reading, literacy, numeracy or a learning difficulty related to either a physical or sensory disability. See Chapter 8: Specific Learning Difficulties.

Statement of Special Educational Needs
A statement of special educational needs is required for those children whose needs are such as to require special educational provision. The statement describes briefly the particular learning difficulties a pupil (a 'statemented child') may have, and sets out the provision which must be made to meet those needs (see also Chapter 9: Questions for Governors).

Support Staff
Personnel in a school who have clerical, technical, medical, welfare, caretaking or supervisory duties (i.e. non-teaching staff). Formerly known as Ancillary Staff; not to be confused with Support Teachers (see below).

Support Teacher
A teacher assigned to work alongside the class teacher either with individual pupils or as part of a project.

3 The Distinctive Rôle of the Church School

In spite of the commitment to integration enshrined in recent government legislation individual schools vary enormously in their thinking and practice. Indeed, many Church schools do not yet have a written policy for special educational needs; they are advised to produce this without delay.

Special educational needs are not solely those which are a reflection of a pupil's inherent difficulties. They can be related to factors within schools which either prevent or exacerbate the problems.

Church schools came into existence (usually as National Schools, with the help of The National Society for Promoting the Education of the Poor in the Principles of the Established Church) to support and to educate those pupils who were poor and disadvantaged. Today the Church continues to play an important rôle in the nation's schooling. It would be impossible to affirm the Christian ethos of a Church school if the manifestation of the Christian faith were not apparent in personal relationships, in admissions policies and in the relationship with the local community. But this ethos must not be taken for granted and it should have regard for the fact that many of our children are growing up speaking more than one language; they visit shops which sell produce from all over the world and the clothes which they wear may reflect cultural and religious diversity. Within a multicultural and multifaith society Church schools should, while remaining true to their Christian foundation, give recognition to a range of cultural and religious perspectives and customs (see ***The Multi-Faith Church School***, Alan Brown, National Society 1992). Children are entitled to learn in an environment where their teachers and parents share common goals on their behalf.

Many children with physical, sensory and emotional or cognitive disorders *are* being educated with skill and devotion but Christians are not immune to prejudices and preconceived ideas about people with special needs. If the Church is the Body of Christ we have a duty to meet the needs of those with exceptional talents as well as young people who encounter learning difficulties both in our schools and in the family of the Church. Good practice is more likely to occur where all members of staff are committed to the same aims. Perhaps the most important consideration is the learning environment which exists within a school. The quality of this environment will depend not only on individual teachers but on the policies and provisions of the headteacher, other members of the school staff, the governing body and in some cases the local education authority. We owe it to the children in our care to create a climate which is *inclusive* of special educational needs; where classrooms are properly organised; where the quality of education is of the highest standard.

Characteristics of a good Church school learning environment:

- a deliberate attempt to link the concerns of the Gospel of Christ with the day-to-day life of the school both in an educational and a spiritual context so that it becomes an expression of God's self-giving love as manifested by Christ in the *kenosis* (Philippians 2.5ff)
- an atmosphere of encouragement, acceptance and respect for achievement and a sensitivity to individual needs in which children's self-esteem and self-confidence grow and in which pupils feel able to risk making mistakes as they learn
- classroom organisation which stimulates pupil/teacher interaction so that children become active learners
- an awareness by all staff of those pupils who have special needs, the nature of these needs and how best to meet these needs
- adequate resources including support and training of staff

- the appointment of a member of staff responsible for coordinating school policy on special educational needs
- flexible groupings of pupils
- a whole school approach to the management of discipline
- co-operative learning amongst pupils
- communication and co-operation between headteacher, teaching staff, governors and parents
- effective management of support from teaching staff, support staff, volunteers and parents
- sensitivity towards the beliefs, hopes and fears of parents and the fostering of a relationship where school and home work in partnership, irrespective of race or creed
- access to specialist advice and support services including child psychologists, speech therapists, health and social services
- co-operation with neighbouring special schools

There is no easy way for the staff or governors of a Church school to address themselves to the task of working out aims and objectives such as these. It is a challenge which the inclusive Gospel of Christ demands of all those who try to live and work to God's praise and glory. Integration will not come spontaneously, nor will it be achieved by legislation alone. It has to be contrived and patiently nurtured. It means positive action in favour of those with special needs, in proportion to the severity of their disabilities, and a recognition of the very positive contribution which children with special educational needs have to make to the life of the school.

4 Responsibilities of Governors

Governors have always had a duty towards all pupils in their schools, but the 1981 Education Act, which was implemented in 1983, spelled out for the first time the specific duties of governors towards children who have special educational needs. Section 2(5) of the Act states:

> 'It shall be the duty of the governors, in the case of a county or voluntary school or a grant-maintained school, and of the local education authority by whom the school is maintained, in the case of a maintained nursery school:
>
> a) to use their best endeavours, in exercising their functions in relation to the school, to secure that if any registered pupil has special educational needs the special educational provision that is required for him is made:
>
> b) to secure that, where the responsible person has been informed by the local education authority that a registered pupil has special educational needs, those needs are made known to all who are likely to teach him; and
>
> c) to secure that the teachers in the school are aware of the importance of identifying, and providing for, those registered pupils who have special educational needs'.

To put this legislation into practice governors will need to ensure that issues concerning special educational needs remain at the heart of their school's planning and development; special educational needs should be a regular agenda item at meetings and included in the headteacher's report. The following should be documented:

A statement in the brochure of the school's commitment and policy towards meeting special educational needs.
Schools will wish to formulate their own prospectus statement concerning their intention to admit and to educate pupils with a wide range of abilities. Obviously factors such as the size and

the physical layout of the school; the expertise of the staff; and the organisation and implementation of the curriculum will all have a part to play and many of the factors discussed in Chapter 3: The Distinctive Rôle of the Church School, might well serve as a starting point for discussion of what should be included in a school policy statement of special educational needs.

Statistics showing the numbers of children in school identified as having special educational needs and the nature of these needs.

Where a child has a statement of special educational needs this will be accompanied by a brief description of the nature of these needs and the learning environment/curriculum requirements. There will also be pupils who have been identified by teaching staff as having more difficulty in learning than would be expected but who have not had a formal assessment of special needs and a statement. It is important that where the school feels able to meet the pupil's needs these children are educated with their peers. LEAs issue policy documents to aid schools in the support of such pupils. All staff should know which pupils have been identified as having special educational needs and the educational implications of these needs.

The system of assessment of all pupils.

A school can function effectively only if it has adopted clear aims and objectives for teaching and learning and ways of assessing pupil achievement. Communicating the extent of these achievements to the children, their parents, colleagues and the wider community is also important. Governors should have access to records of children's progress.

Support offered to pupils with learning difficulties.

There is wide variation in the practice of LEAs regarding the policy and provision made for pupils with special educational needs. Governors should make it their responsibility to obtain the current policy document from the LEA and to ensure that the school receives adequate multi-professional support for both statemented and non-statemented children. Every child with a statement of special educational needs is entitled to the provision outlined in that statement and to the support of appropriate professional services (including educational psychologists, physiotherapists, speech therapists and medical personnel).

Communication with parents.
The relationship between parents and the school which their child is attending has a crucial bearing upon the child's educational progress. If parents are to support the efforts of teachers they need information and advice from the school. There can be no substitute for personal access of parents to a school whenever they require information or to discuss a child's progress. Governors should encourage headteachers to welcome parents on a regular informal basis. A child's special needs cannot be adequately assessed and met without the insights which parents are able to provide. Parents can be kept informed in various ways. Schools must give parents information about the type of curriculum which their child is following and this information must also be included in the school brochure. The annual governors' report to parents and the annual parents' meeting provide an opportunity for discussion and for raising questions.

Staff training on special educational needs.
A school's staff is its major resource; governors should encourage and support staff training programmes organised within and outside school. When teachers are released from school to attend courses and training sessions, a brief outline of these should be documented by the headteacher and included in the annual report.

Liaison with specialist support agencies including educational psychologists, social services, and advisers.
A child's statement of special educational needs will include details of any specialist support which the pupil should receive in order that his/her special needs may be met. LEAs now incorporate some form of multi-professional assessment in the identification of children with special educational needs and it

is the duty of the LEA to ensure that any recommended support is forthcoming.

Although it is unusual for personnel from support services to be included in the full-time staff of a mainstream school their contribution and expertise should not be overlooked. Inviting them to a governors' meeting to outline their rôle will not only make them feel valued but also encourage the idea of partnership in education.

Links with special schools.
At a time when there are fewer opportunities available for in-service training mainstream schools will do well to develop links with a local special school and to arrange exchange visits and invite staff to lead training days.. Where partnerships have been established it is not uncommon for staff from both schools to remark on the likenesses rather than the differences in children's learning. Indeed a primary school may often have far more in common with the special school next door than a mainstream primary school in another area. Governors should include accounts of initiatives such as these in the annual report to parents and in the school policy statement of special educational needs.

5 Parents as Partners in their Child's Education

Governors may be called upon at any time to give advice and support to parents and it is their duty to familiarise themselves with relevant legislation. They are strongly advised to make reference to the books and sources of information listed in Chapter 11: A Guide to Documents Concerning Special Educational Needs.

The Process

Parents who believe their child may have special educational needs can ask for him/her to be assessed and this request must be complied with unless the LEA believes it to be unreasonable. (DES *Circular 8/81* para 22). The assessment process must not take longer than six months from the delivery of a draft statement (which should be written in straightforward style in a language with which parents are familiar or for which they are able to obtain an interpreter). Parents have a right to a copy of all the advice obtained when a statement of special educational needs is made and this advice must be attached as part of the statement which is sent to the parents in draft form at the end of the assessment.

The advice given to parents should contain the following information:

- the educational, psychological, medical or other factors which are pertinent to the child's educational needs both at present and in the future
- how these factors could affect the child's educational needs
- the educational and other provision which will be required in order that the child may benefit from the special education detailed

There are several items which an LEA also has the duty to inform parents about once a decision has been made to assess a child:

- a proposal to assess the child, with a brief explanation of the reason
- a summary of the procedures to be followed
- the name of an officer in the LEA who will give parents more information
- the time and place of the assessment and a statement of parents' rights to attend
- a statement regarding the right of parents to make representations about the proposals

Parents have the right to appeal, at two stages, against a statement of their child's special educational needs. The first occurs under section 5(6), where the LEA has carried out an assessment of a child (under section 5 of the 1981 Act) but decides that a statement of special educational needs is not required, the parent can appeal to The Secretary of State. The Secretary of State may direct the LEA to reconsider its decision. Secondly, where the parents disagree with the special educational provision set out in a statement, (under section 8 of the 1981 Act), they may appeal to an appeals committee, arranged by the LEA in accordance with the provisions of the Education Act 1980. The appeals committee may confirm this statement or refer it back to the LEA for reconsideration. The appeals committee's decisions are not however binding and parents have the right to appeal direct to the Secretary of State if they are dissatisfied with the decision. It is expected that under the 1993 Education Bill an independent tribunal will take over from the Secretary of State and the appeals committee the rôle of hearing appeals at either stage.

School/Parent Communication

In Chapter 4: Responsibilities of Governors, one of the topics discussed is communication with parents. The following check list builds on some of the ideas already discussed and suggests some areas which the headteacher and governors might consider when they are formulating a school policy which includes parents as partners in their child's education

Linking with home
- home visits by teaching staff and support services
- parent representation on the governing body
- home-based learning and school curriculum follow-up
- learning and behaviour management programmes at home and school

Parents in school
- visiting classes during the school day and attending assemblies
- assisting in children's learning e.g. hearing children read, helping during swimming/sports, wider curriculum areas
- parent/teacher projects
- adult education classes for parents and others

Topics for meetings
Case conferences
Annual reviews
Links with the governing body
Multi-disciplinary links
Parent-teacher partnership
School curriculum
Written communication
School brochure
School notice board
School curriculum
Newsletters in appropriate languages
Home diaries
Record-keeping at home and school

6 The School Curriculum and Assessment of Children's Progress

Children's learning takes place anywhere, everywhere, at any time. At the heart of this section of the booklet lies the philosophy that *all* children have individual needs in learning and that the teaching force in any one school can manage planning, organisation and teaching methods to meet these needs.

The National Curriculum is an entitlement for all children, with or without a statement of special educational needs. The National Curriculum Council states that the right to share in the National Curriculum does not however ensure access to it or progress within it. Indeed the Education Reform Act contained provision for all or part of the National Curriculum requirements to be modified or removed for some children. Parents, governors and LEAs must be informed of the exclusion of a child from any part of the curriculum; governors are strongly advised to look closely at the way that the National Curriculum is implemented in their school and to consider whether the lack of access of some pupils to it might be an indication that it is being too rigidly interpreted. (See Chapter 9: Questions for Governors.)

Children with special educational needs may have access to the National Curriculum in four ways:

- with a modified teaching approach, although the content itself remains unchanged
- with some modification; e.g. pupils with sensory impairment may need to learn skills such as typing in Braille or extra language work
- with significant modification which aims to make available as much of the mainstream curriculum as

possible but takes into account the pupil's individual needs and capacities
- with additions which have an emphasis on a child's individual needs, particularly social and life skills

At present there is widespread concern that *all* pupils should have access to the National Curriculum and questions about the breadth, balance and coherence of the curriculum have figured prominently in the debates of educationalists. School governors share with LEAs, teaching and support services a responsibility for providing a curriculum which 'promotes the spiritual, moral, cultural, mental and physical development of pupils at the school and of society' and 'prepares such pupils for the opportunities, responsibilities and experiences of adult life'.

The Education Reform Act 1988 endorsed the following points concerning the content of a curriculum, regardless of the ability of the pupils for whom it is designed. It should be:

BROAD: introducing children to a wide range of knowledge, understanding and skills.

BALANCED: each part should be allotted enough time for it to make a worthwhile contribution to education as a whole.

RELEVANT: to the present and future needs of children, giving due emphasis to practical aspects.

DIFFERENTIATED: what is taught and how it is taught should be matched to the ability and aptitude of the children.

For staff working with pupils with special educational needs, the implementation and application of the National Curriculum can be a challenge. Access to National Curriculum subjects alone cannot meet all the needs of pupils. The whole curriculum should seek to do this. The National Curriculum Council document *Curriculum Guidance 3* (1990) defined the whole curriculum as comprising:

- core and foundation subjects
- religious education
- additional subjects beyond the ten subjects of the National Curriculum
- cross-curricular elements
- extra-curricular activities

Teachers of children with special educational needs are aware that what their pupils require more than anything else is to know that they are accepted and that they should be given the kind of encouragement in their learning which is an expression of other people's faith in them. Instead of perceiving a child as 'failing' the curriculum we need to enable him or her to reach realistic and achievable learning goals through providing a rich and diverse bank of educational experiences. For the least able children this may mean choosing those areas of the curriculum which they enjoy and which they are motivated to participate in. For children with profound and multiple learning difficulties, the application of the National Curriculum can challenge fundamental principles and existing practice. The scale of this challenge to teachers should not be underestimated. Nevertheless, entitlement to a 'curriculum for all' applies to these pupils as it does to any others.

If pupils with special needs are to be educated adequately in mainstream schools these educational needs should be considered and met within a whole-school context so that each child has equal, though uniquely differing, access to the curriculum and other opportunities offered by the school.

Assessing Children's Progress

The Education Reform Act 1988 requires all schools by law to keep a record of children's progress. Since September 1989 governing bodies have been required to keep records of every child registered in the school. These records must be updated at least once a year and parents of registered pupils under the age of eighteen and pupils of sixteen and over have the right to see their educational records. For pupils with a statement of special educational needs, LEAs must review the child's statement in the light of his/her progress and how the educational provision is made to meet the child's special educational needs annually (Education Act 1981). A reassessment of a child's statement of special educational needs may also be made at this time. Reviews are usually based on reports prepared by the school the child attends including (where appropriate) the views of teachers and other professionals who work with the child. The assessments made under the 1988 Act with reference to the National Curriculum should also be included and whilst there is no specific duty to involve parents in an annual review it would be unreasonable of a school not to do so.

The rôle of the classroom teacher in recording children's progress

Recording the progress of children with special educational needs can be a daunting task. It will often take place as part of the teacher's day-to-day observance of pupils, noting the questions they ask and observing their actions. The teacher's rôle is to listen and to prompt in such a way as to encourage children to take further steps in their thinking and their response. The rôle also extends beyond that of the formal assessment of the child to a self-evaluation by classroom teachers. Asking some of the following questions is a valuable exercise:

- Am I showing concern for each pupil as an individual, encouraging sensitivity towards others and the forming of relationships?
- Does my teaching approach give children ample opportunity to explore their own experience?
- Am I giving sufficient opportunity for pupil participation and does my teaching encourage children to ask questions and to express themselves?

- Does my teaching provide rich opportunities for the development of listening, language and thinking skills (where appropriate)?
- Do I show an appreciation of every child's contribution, letting them know that effort is more important than success?
- Have the children gained enjoyment from their learning?
- Am I creating a climate of mutual respect for the varied social, cultural and religious differences of the children within my class?
- Do I take the time to observe and know the children and to build a rapport with each child?
- How successful am I in keeping records of children's development and progress?
- Do these enable me to ensure continuity and progression in the educational experiences I provide for each child?
- What particular strengths and expertise have I as a teacher which could help other colleagues?

It is a sobering fact that a child's view of what happens in the classroom is sometimes quite different from that of the teacher. As a profession we often think that we are providing a learning situation or that what we are saying is clear and easy to grasp. Yet how often do children's reactions reveal that what they have absorbed is something very different from that which was intended? However schools choose to plan and assess the school curriculum and the progress of their pupils they should set themselves high standards. In this way neither the content of the curriculum nor the development of the children will remain static. It will change and develop.

7 School Staffing

A school's staff is its major resource. The success of children's learning will depend largely on the quality of the relationship between teachers, support staff and pupils. It will demand an intimate knowledge and understanding of the children: their strengths and their weaknesses, different levels of emotional and physical maturity and the influence of home and family. Pupils learn far more from the people who surround them than they do from formal education.

Of all things which affect the way in which children learn, the most important yet difficult to describe is the atmosphere that exists in a school, and especially the relationship between all those who work in classrooms where children are expected to commit themselves in a personal way and where their responses are exposed to the view of others. Governors and staff should ensure that the school's ethos (for example, the Christian ethos of a Church school) is reflected in the attitudes and values of all who work there.

Specialist teachers

Teachers and headteachers are often expected to be familiar with ranges of learning difficulty but they cannot be experts on the whole variety of special educational needs. The appointment of a teacher with a knowledge of special educational needs and experience of teaching 'special' children will go a long way to ensuring a successful programme of integration in a mainstream school.

Recruiting

Because of the variety of skills and responsibilities associated with the post and the wide-ranging demands, several considerations must be borne in mind: the designated teacher should have proven classroom experience; the wide-ranging responsibilities involved in the rôle must be reflected in the status of the post; the extent of the responsibilities must be clearly defined from the outset to avoid misunderstandings on the part of other colleagues.

Outlining responsibilities
Responsibilities might include:

- assessment of children on admission to school and regular recording of achievement
- devising pupil programmes of work
- modification of the school curriculum so that it is accessible to all pupils
- supporting mainstream colleagues, within and outside the classroom
- liaison with feeder schools or secondary schools
- regular time-tabled teaching of mainstream classes
- providing opportunities for staff development in the area of special needs
- liaison with external agencies e.g. educational psychologists, social workers, speech therapists, physiotherapists

Some questions to ask at the interview

[In a Church school] What do you consider to be the distinctive contribution which a Church school has to make to the education of pupils with special educational needs?

In the light of your initial visit to school, can you tell the interviewing panel about the skills and expertise you feel you are able to offer to the school's programme of integration?

Why do you consider an ability to work closely with teaching colleagues and support personnel is important?

Can you tell the panel about any past experience you have in leading staff development training in special needs?

How might you support colleagues inside and outside the classroom?

Do you consider it important that your approach to teaching pupils with special educational needs should fully explore the potential in the classroom, the school, the local community [and the church family]?

Support staff

Many pupils with special needs benefit from a degree of caring support. This will range from helping children with physical disabilities in getting around school, to toileting, giving medication and checking the arrival and departure of pupils.

The school's support staff are a valuable resource for any integration programme. Whilst their rôle is to provide a level of support that frees teachers to concentrate on teaching, there will be times when support staff are actively involved in children's learning experiences. For this reason the selection of support staff should be carried out with the same care as that of teaching staff.

Some questions to ask at the interview

Can you tell the interviewing panel your reasons for applying for the post?

Do you consider an ability to work closely with teaching colleagues is important?

Can you tell the panel about any past experience you have had working with children?

Can you tell the panel about any experience you may have already had working with children with special educational needs?

In-service Training/Staff Development

The Warnock Report recognised that ordinary teachers would require further training if they were to provide an adequate education for pupils with special needs in mainstream schools. The growth of in-service training for special educational needs was phenomenal in the decade which followed, but since the Education Reform Act 1988 and the implementation of the National Curriculum it has not been forthcoming on anything like the scale required. As a result, many schools are organising their own training sessions and those staff with a special education background may be in a position to share knowledge with their mainstream colleagues.

For schools beginning to plan in-service training/staff development which will increase knowledge and expertise of special educational needs, the following suggestions are offered:

- prepare and discuss case studies of children in school; use these as examples for curriculum planning, classroom organisation etc.
- liaise with a local special school
- study aspects of special education, including resumes of relevant research, articles and books
- invite persons with expertise in special education to lead training sessions/workshops
- raise awareness and develop knowledge of special education, curriculum approaches, support services
- study the implications of special educational needs for children's learning.

8 Pupils with Specific Learning Difficulties

In this section a brief outline is given of some of the more common types of sensory and physical disability, with possible implications for school organisation and teaching. Governors and teachers are recommended to liaise closely with support services, colleagues in special schools, and organisations which may be contacted through the Council for Disabled Children (see page 51); these are sources of more detailed information.

Types of Disability
Auditory Disabilities

Deafness is a hidden disability and there is a wide variety of degree and type of hearing loss. Hearing is not absolute. Deafness is rarely total. Estimates by different authorities vary, but most agree that at most only two per cent of children with hearing deficiencies have no hearing whatsoever.

A profoundly deaf person is usually understood to be someone whose disability precludes him/her from processing linguistic information through the sense of hearing.

Visual Impairment

People with visual disabilities are often referred to as 'blind', 'partially seeing' or 'visually handicapped', with the underlying assumption that they are a homogeneous group. In fact they are no more homogeneous than any group of seeing individuals. Not all visually impaired people are totally without sight. Some can perceive differences in light and shade; others will have images which are distorted, blurred or fragmentary. Some people will have started life with normal vision and will have a store of visual memories until an accident, infection, tumour or degenerative condition leads to loss of sight.

Distance vision is usually stated according to what can be seen on the Snellen Chart (the familiar long chart with letters on it). Normal vision is stated as 20/20, which means that a person sees what he or she is supposed to see at a distance of twenty feet with that eye.

Any person whose vision (in the better eye) cannot be corrected with spectacles to more than 20/200 is considered to be legally blind.

Physical Disability

There is a tremendous range of physical disability. Some defects are congenital and some are acquired as a result of accident or disease after birth. Some disabilities are mild and transitory, others are permanent, incapacitating and result in premature death. Physical disabilities may be put into in four main categories:

Congenital Conditions / Malformations
It has been estimated that possibly six per cent of the population have a congenital defect which is noticed by the first year of life. Such conditions include dislocation of the hip, which can be corrected, and moderate or severe malformation of the face, head or limbs.

Neurological Impairment
One of the most common causes of physical disability is damage to the central nervous system, i.e. the spinal cord or the brain. Brain damage may occur in the area of the brain controlling major coordination, or the spinal cord may be damaged so that nervous impulses will no longer be sent to the brain. When the nervous system is damaged, muscular weakness or paralysis is a likely consequence. Cerebral palsy, epilepsy, hydrocephalus, multiple sclerosis and spina bifida are disabilities in this category.

Musculo-Skeletal Disorders
These are defects or diseases of the muscles or bones. They include arthritis and different types of muscular dystrophy.

Disabilities as a Result of Accidents or Disease
Children may suffer from head injuries or limb loss as a result of an accident, and mild or serious physical disability may be caused by conditions such as asthma, haemophilia, leukaemia or sickle cell disease.

Organising the Classroom
Pupils with auditory impairment
Children with hearing impairment should sit where they are able to make the most of what is seen and heard in the room. This means that, where possible they should be within 2-3 metres of the teacher, and slightly to one side with the light source behind other class members in order that they are able to turn to face a person who might be talking and to see them clearly.

Before a pupil with hearing impairment is admitted to a school classroom teachers should have a basic understanding of the nature of hearing loss. They should also be au fait with hearing aids and able to check that they are functioning properly. Likewise pupils should have had some training in the development of listening skills.

Pupils with visual impairment
Most classroom situations require children to be constantly changing their visual attention and children with visual impairment may have difficulty maintaining this. There will also be considerable individual differences in the way in which impaired sight affects children's understanding of their environment.

Lighting is of tremendous importance to children who use sighted methods of learning. All pupils should of course learn in rooms which are adequately lit but differing visual difficulties demand different kinds of lighting. In most schools where the source of natural light is not adequate this may be supplemented by artificial light and problems of glare may be controlled by the use of blinds and seating arrangements.

Many children with moderate visual impairment find that the best place for them to sit is in a central position and in a traditionally arranged classroom. Pupils with severe or profound visual impairment often prefer to sit at the side of the room or towards the back of a traditionally organised classroom so that the walls give an easy point of reference.

Following some additional organisational points for pupils with severe visual impairment will aid integration enormously and cost very little:

- any changes of room layout should be followed by a re-orientation session so that children are able to continue movement with confidence
- classroom doors should be always fully open or completely shut
- there should be no obstructions e.g. bags left in the aisles or spaces between desks and tables
- whiteboards are easier than blackboards for partially-sighted persons to read
- matt finishes on walls, ceilings and floors prevent glare and reflection

Pupils with Other Physical Disabilities

For pupils in wheelchairs independence of movement and social interaction is more easily achieved in a large open-plan room. Questions of furniture and pupil mobility are not restricted to those in wheelchairs, however. Other physical disabilities require specialist equipment: items such as power points for desk lamps, shelves and cupboards for storing Braille machines.

Where aids to learning are introduced into a classroom they should be as unobtrusive as possible so they do not constitute a physical barrier which separates pupils with special educational needs from the rest of the class. In primary classrooms where the pupils tend to be based in one place the teacher will have much greater control over this than in the secondary school setting where there is much greater frequency of movement from one place to the next.

The provision, replacement and servicing of equipment is also an issue and schools should ensure that from the beginning of a policy of integration this is included in the budget.

It is recommended that no child with a physical disability should be admitted into school before the following check list is completed.

- As much information as possible should be obtained before admission. If possible the child should be visited in his/her feeder school or home.
- All staff should be aware of the educational/organisational and social implications of the child's special need.
- Physical adaptations to the classroom/school should be made.
- Emergency procedures should be anticipated and made known to the staff concerned.
- Help, support and guidance from outside agencies should be sought and encouraged.
- The mobility of the pupil should be fully assessed (if appropriate) and physiotherapy arranged if necessary.

Glossary of Terms

This list is not definitive. It represents the terminology most commonly used in statements of special educational needs, in school medical reports and by support services working with disabled children.

Acheiria   Absence of a hand.

Accommodation The adjustment of the eye for seeing at varying distances.

Adactylia   Absence of fingers.

Adventitious Describes a disability which was not present at birth but has since occurred through accident or illness.

Agnosia   Inability to recognise familiar objects by sight.

Albinism   A lack of pigment in the hair, skin and eyes which is often associated with defective vision.

Amelia	Absence of a limb.
Amnesia	Loss of memory.
Anaemia	Lack of haemoglobin or oxygen carrying cells in the blood.
Aphakia	The absence of the lens of the eye.
Aphasia	A loss or impairment of the ability to express oneself through speech, writing or signs or an inability to comprehend spoken or written language as the result of congenital or adventitious brain damage (see above).
Apodia	Absence of a foot.
Arthritis	A disease suffered by about one child in 1,500, it is more prevalent in girls than in boys and its cause is still unknown. Some kinds of arthritis affect the spine, others cause extreme pain and stiffness, for example in the small joints of the hand.
Asthma	An intermittent condition, rather than a permanent disability, which narrows the breathing tubes or airways of the lungs. Attacks can be frightening both for the child and for the onlooker.
Ataxia	Lack of muscular coordination.
Athetosis	Athetosis is characterised by involuntary writhing, jerky, uncoordinated movements. About 25% of cerebral palsied children are athetoids.
Audiologist	A professional person skilled in the identification and measurement of hearing loss.
Audiometry	The technique of measuring the sense of hearing by means of instrumentation.

Binaural — Amplification provided to both ears, each receiving sound from separate input sources.

Biopsy — Removal of a small piece of tissue for examination in order to make a diagnosis.

Body Aid — A hearing aid worn on the chest.

Bone Conduction — The transmission of sound pressure waves through the bones of the inner ear.

Cataract — An opacity of the lens of the eye resulting in blurred vision. Cataracts may be congenital or adventitious.

Central Deafness — Deafness due to the inability of the brain to recognise or to process sounds.

Cerebral Palsy — The term 'spastic' is commonly used to describe this condition, although spasticity is just one of a number of cerebral palsies. Motor problems are often accompanied by intellectual impairment and speech and sensory disorders.

Cognitive — Pertaining to the mental processes of perceiving and conceiving; of knowing and comprehending.

Conductive Deafness — A type of deafness caused by a 'blockage' or abnormal hindrance to vibration and the transmission of sound in the outer or middle ear. Generally conductive deafness results in a partial rather than a severe degree of hearing loss.

Congenital — Existing at birth, but not necessarily inherited.

Convergence — The coordinated movement of both eyes towards fixation on the same near point.

Cystic Fibrosis — An inherited disease characterised by chronic digestive and respiratory problems.

Depth Perception	The ability to perceive the relative position of an object in space.
Dialysis	Purification of blood by causing it to flow through a suitable membrane.
Diplegia	Paralysis of symmetrical parts.
Distance Senses	Vision and hearing.
Dysmelia	Having an imperfect or faulty limb.
Epilepsy	Seizures caused by an abnormal discharge of electrical activity in the brain. Some fits are mild and may appear to be mere lapses of concentration: others are severe. Epilepsy affects children across the whole range of ability.
Glaucoma	A disease of the eye characterised by: increased pressure of fluid within the eyeball, which may in turn exert pressure on the retina and the optic nerve; blurred vision; loss of peripheral vision before loss of central vision; pain in the eyes.
Haemoglobin	The red oxygen carrying substance in the blood.
Haemophilia	A rare disorder of the blood which is transmitted through a recessive gene carried by the mother. Only boys suffer from most forms. There are no learning difficulties specifically associated with this condition although children will rarely be able to play competitive sport. The majority of children with haemophilia cope well in ordinary schools.
Hemiplegia	Paralysis of the arm and leg on the same side of the body.
Hydro-cephalus	An enlargement of the head which is due to interference with the circulation and absorption of the cerebro-spinal fluid which

surrounds the brain and the spinal cord. Where hydrocephalus occurs there is a likelihood of mental disability.

Kidney Disorders — Anaemia and tiredness are common to kidney disorders and, where kidneys function inadequately and waste products accumulate in the blood, the child may become irritable and sometimes confused.

Leukaemia — A term given to a group of diseases in which there is a malignant change in the bone marrow. Leukaemia is the most common form of childhood cancer and it is estimated that there are approximately 360 new cases in Britain each year. Treatment for leukaemia is intensive and sometimes debilitating in the early stages: some children may experience changes in their physical appearance, most commonly an increase in weight or the loss of all or most of their hair. The psychological effects of this change in appearance must not be underestimated.

Loss of Limb — Children may be born without a limb, or part of one, or they may lose all or part of a limb as the result of an accident. There are no specific learning difficulties associated with loss of limb, but for some children multiple limb loss may present serious implications for their mobility and curriculum design.

Malignant — Harmful cells, cancerous cells which grow abnormally and rapidly.

Multiple Sclerosis — A slowly progressive disease of the central nervous system where there is hardening or scarring of the protective sheath around certain nerves.

Muscular Dystrophy	There are several types of muscular dystrophy, all of which are progressive, hereditary diseases. The main characteristic of the disease is the progressive breakdown and death of muscle fibre which results in gradually increasing weakness.
Myopia	A condition where the eyeball is too long from front to back resulting in near-sightedness.
Neurological	Connected with the nervous system.
Neural Tube	The tube of cells in embrological development from which the brain and spinal cord develop.
Ophthalmologist	A physician who specialises in the diagnosis and treatment of diseases of the eye, performing surgery when necessary or prescribing other types of treatment including spectacles.
Optician	A person who tests sight, grinds lenses, fits them into frames and adjusts the frames to the wearer.
Optometrist	A licensed non-medical practitioner who measures refractive errors, e.g. irregularities in the size or shape of the eyeball or surface of the cornea.
Orthosis	Splint for a disabled part of the body.
Osteotomy	Division of bone or removal of section of bone.
Perception	The learned ability to register consciously, or give meaning to sensory stimulus.
Photophobia	Extreme sensitivity to light.
Physiotherapy	Treatment by massage and/or exercises.
Prosthesis	An artificial substitute for a part of the body which is absent or which has been surgically removed.

Residual Vision	The potential remaining vision which the person may be able to utilise.
Retinal Detachment	A separation of the retina from the choroid.
Rubella	A congenital syndrome caused by intra-uterine rubella infection (German Measles).
Sensori-neural Disorder	A type of deafness caused by damage to the cochlea or nerves of hearing. Sensori-neural deafness varies in degree from mild to total loss.
Sickle Cell Disease	An inherited disability affecting the haemoglobin factor in the blood. Most children with sickle cell disease will be able to attend school regularly but their education may be interrupted by sickle cell crisis and require hospital treatment.
Spasticity	Spasticity affects about 50-60% of children with cerebral palsy. Spastic children commonly have increased muscle tone and rigid limbs which results in poor posture.
Spina Bifida	When spina bifida occurs, the bones of the spine are not closed completely and the nerves and/or their protective sheathing are exposed.
Spinal Injury after Birth	Any injury to the spinal cord caused by accident or illness results in loss of movement and feeling. Children with spinal injuries do not usually have any intellectual impairment.
Syndrome	A recognisable collection of abnormal features or symptoms.
Tactile	Pertaining to touch.
Usher's Syndrome	A genetically transmitted disease which results in profound congenital hearing loss.

9 Questions for Governors

What is a Statement of Special Educational Needs?
A statement of special educational needs describes briefly the particular learning difficulties a pupil may have, and sets out the provision which must be made to meet those needs. The school which the pupil will attend is usually named, together with details of any additional support the child should receive. Both the child's parents and the LEA are bound by the special educational provision written in the statement which is subject to an annual review and may be amended as appropriate.

When is a Statement of Special Educational Needs made?
The statement is made after a child has been identified either by parents, school, health authority or social services as having special educational needs. A multi-professional assessment of the child is made, and it must involve the parents and their views. The statement may be made before a child starts school or at any time during compulsory schooling.

Does the LEA have a responsibility for the training of school governors concerning special educational needs?
Under the 1986 Education Act, LEAs are required to provide training for school governors but there is no specific guidance concerning special educational needs. Governing bodies should therefore request training concerning special education.

What is my rôle as a governor in relation to children 'statemented' as having special educational needs?
Much of the background information to this question will be found within the text of the booklet. In brief, you have a duty to ensure the following:

- all staff are aware of the child's special educational needs
- the provision specified on the statement is met
- the progress of the child is fully monitored
- parents are kept fully informed and involved

- the child is integrated as fully as possible into all aspects of school life

What about children without a statement of special educational needs?

Formal 'statementing' of a child's special educational needs is not required if a school is able to provide extra resources in the form of teaching and support for a child who has learning difficulties. There is wide variation in the practice of LEAs regarding policy and provision for special educational needs.

DES *Circular 1/83* recommended that LEAs should issue guidance to all maintained schools in 'identifying, assessing and meeting special educational needs'. It is worthwhile consulting your LEA for its most recent policy document on special educational needs.

Does a child with special educational needs have to follow the National Curriculum?

The National Curriculum was introduced to all schools in 1989 but this has taken place in stages. The exclusion of a child from all or part of the National Curriculum is at the discretion of the headteacher. There are two kinds of 'direction' which can be made:

- a general direction in cases where the headteacher believes that a child's difficulties are only temporary
- a special direction when the headteacher believes that the pupil's difficulties are such that a full assessment under the 1981 Education Act 1981 should be made. Any such exclusion must not exceed six months (although it can be renewed) and the headteacher must be able to show how the school proposes to re-integrate a pupil into the National Curriculum and whether the pupil will be subject to an assessment or statement of her/his needs. Parents, governors and LEAs must be informed of the exclusion of a child from any part of the curriculum and parents have the right to appeal to the governing body if they disagree with the headteacher's

decision to make, change or revoke a direction. On appeal, the governing body can confirm the headteacher's action or direct him/her to do anything which it regards as appropriate and which is in line with the regulations. The governing body must inform the headteacher in writing and he/she must comply. If a parent is not satisfied with the direction of the governing body a complaint may be made either through the LEA or, in the case of a grant-maintained school, through its procedure. Further details may be found in Sections 19 and 23 of the Education Reform Act 1988.

Governors are strongly advised to look closely at the way in which the National Curriculum is implemented in their school and to consider whether the exclusion of pupils from its application might be an indication that it is being too rigidly interpreted.

Who is directly responsible in a school for giving information about a child when an assessment of special educational needs is requested?
Educational information about a child will normally be sought from the headteacher of a school attended by the child within the last eighteen months, or if this is not possible, from a qualified teacher whom the LEA is satisfied has experience of teaching children with special educational needs. Headteachers who have not personally taught the child within the last eighteen months must consult with a teacher who has, before giving information. For children who are thought to have a visual or hearing impairment the advice must be given by persons qualified to teach such children, or after consultation with someone suitably qualified.

What happens if after assessing a child the LEA decides not to make a Statement of Special Educational Needs?
If the LEA decides after the assessment of a child that a statement of her/his special educational needs is not necessary the parents must be informed in writing and told that they have

a right of appeal to an independent tribunal, which can direct the LEA to reconsider.

To whom may a statement of a child's special educational needs be made available?

Statements must not be shown to persons who are not directly concerned with the education of a child unless parental consent is given. Statements should be kept where unauthorised people do not have access to them. This also applies to any advice or information which has been provided to an LEA and which forms part of the statement. Education (Special Educational Needs) Regulations 1983 allow disclosure, without parental consent, of a statement of special educational needs to the following:

- persons to whom the LEA believes the statement should be shown 'in the educational interests of the child'
- for appeals to local appeal committees or tribunals
- by court order or, 'for the purpose of any criminal proceedings'
- for research, provided nothing published reveals the identity of the child or the parents and that the research is likely to contribute to the education of children with special educational needs
- for purposes of investigation by the Local Government Ombudsman

What are the financial implications of admitting statemented children to a school?

Integrating pupils with special educational needs has a financial implication for schools and it is important that these costs are acknowledged, identified, and realistically addressed. A separate budget for children with special educational needs, including the cost of educational support, will need to be drawn up. It is the duty of school governors to explore with LEAs the extra resources which will be made available to a school in respect of admitting pupils who are statemented as having special educational needs.

10 Recent Government Policy for Special Educational Needs

It is very important to remember that the provisions of the 1981 Education Act still stand alongside those of the Education Reform Act 1988. The 1981 Act changed both policy and provision; it endorsed the idea that 'special educational needs' is a relative concept describing a continuum from greater to lesser educational needs. For many people the most significant part of the 1981 Act was that which promoted (for the first time) the education of children with special educational needs in ordinary schools alongside pupils without such needs, rather than in separate schools. This Act endorsed most of the recommendations of the Warnock Report (see page 5).

The 1988 Education Reform Act appeared to mark new ground for pupils with special educational needs. It stated that *all* pupils share the same rights to a broad and balanced curriculum, including access to the National Curriculum.

The Parents' Charter: You and Your Child's Education (1992) explained to parents of children with special educational needs their rights and how to exercise them; it included an explanation of LEA procedures for making assessments and statements of special education needs. According to ***The Parents' Charter*** the Government will legislate to:

- extend parents' rights to the choice of school
- reduce the time taken by LEAs in making assessments and statements of special educational needs
- make parents' rights to appeal more coherent, and extend those rights
- establish an independent tribunal to hear appeals under the Education Act 1981.

The 1993 Education Bill remains firmly committed to the principle, enshrined in the 1981 Act, that pupils with special educational needs should be educated in ordinary schools wherever possible. It also includes the following proposals:

- LEAs will retain their responsibilities for assessments and statements of special educational needs under the Education Act 1981.
- Any maintained school named in a child's statement of special educational needs will be required to admit the child.
- The LEA and the Funding Agency will, from the 10% entry point, share the duty to secure sufficient places in the area for pupils with statements of special educational needs.
- The Secretary of State will have power to make regulations to enable special schools to apply for grant-maintained status.
- The Secretary of State will have power to require LEAs or the Funding Agency to bring forward proposals for prescribed alterations to special schools.
- The Secretary of State will also have power to put forward his/her own proposals and the alternative sets of proposals will be open to a public inquiry.

In many ways recent legislation has failed to take into account the dilemma faced by mainstream schools in attempting to integrate pupils with special educational needs. It is a sad fact that many of these children could be perceived to 'fail' within mainstream education. This should not happen, however, in Church schools and others if governors are fully aware of their responsibilities and use their powers to influence, in a positive way, the educational standards which headteachers and staff are striving to achieve.

11 Guide to Documents Concerning Special Educational Needs

The Education Act 1981
The Act concerned the provision made for the education of pupils with special educational needs. It received Royal Assent on 30 October 1981 and all sections were in force by 1 April 1983.

Education (Schools Information) Regulations 1981
This contained information about special educational provision in LEAs and individual schools which must be made available to parents.

DES Circular 8/81
This explained the basic provisions of the Act.

Education (Special Educational Needs) Regulations 1983
These contained detailed provisions on the assessment and statementing of children with special educational needs and came into force on 1 April 1983.

Education (No. 2) Act 1986
This introduced new responsibilities for school governors.

Education Reform Act 1988
This introduced wide-ranging changes in what was to be taught in schools and in the management of schools.

DES Circular 15/89
This discussed in detail the implications of the National Curriculum for pupils with SEN.

DES Circular 22/89 Assessments and Statements of Special Educational Needs
This was a joint circular with the DHSS (Health Circular 83/3) and Local Authorities (Circular LAC (83)2) which contained advice on Assessments and Statements.

DES Parents' Charter 1992
Outlined basic facts about parental rights and those of children with SEN including rights to appeal against statements.

DFE Special Educational Needs – Access to the System 1992
A consultation document outlining the Government's proposals to amend the Education Act 1981.

The Education Act 1993
(When published.)

Organisations Concerned With Special Educational Needs

There is a growing number of voluntary organisations which offer help and guidance concerning the education and welfare of children with special educational needs. The list is long, and changes occur rapidly. Up-to-date details of any of these organisations may be obtained from:

>The Council for Disabled Children,
>National Children's Bureau,
>8 Wakley Street,
>London ECIV 7QE
>Telephone 071-278 9441 Fax 071-278 9512

National Society Publications

The National Society's range of publications includes a series of booklets on religious education, school worship, pastoral issues and Church school management. Full details of these and other publications can be found in the resources catalogue available from the Society at the address on page 52.

The National Society

The National Society (Church of England) for Promoting Religious Education is the voluntary body, founded in 1811, which established the first network of schools in England and Wales based on the National Church. It now supports all those involved in Christian Education – diocesan education teams, teachers, governors, clergy, students and parents – with the resources of its RE Centres, archives, courses and conferences. The Society publishes a wide range of books, pamphlets, audio-visual items, and two magazines; ***Crosscurrent*** and ***Together***. It can give legal and administrative advice to schools and colleges and award grants for Church school building projects.

The Society works in close association with the General Synod Board of Education and with the Division of Education of the Church in Wales, but greatly values the independent status which enables it to take initiatives in developing new work. The Society has a particular concern for Christian goals and values in education as a whole.

For a resources catalogue and details of corporate, associate and individual membership of the Society contact:

> The Promotions Secretary,
> The National Society,
> Church House,
> Great Smith Street,
> London SW1P 3NZ
> Telephone: 071-222 1672
> Fax: 071-233 2592